AF576697

AUSTRALIAN ART MASTERS

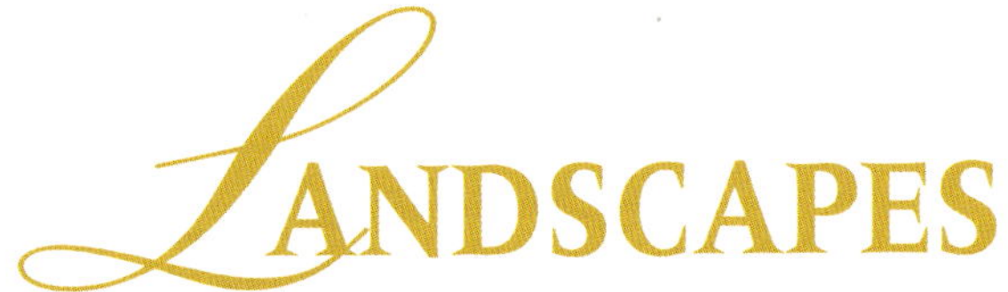

ELIZABETH STUART

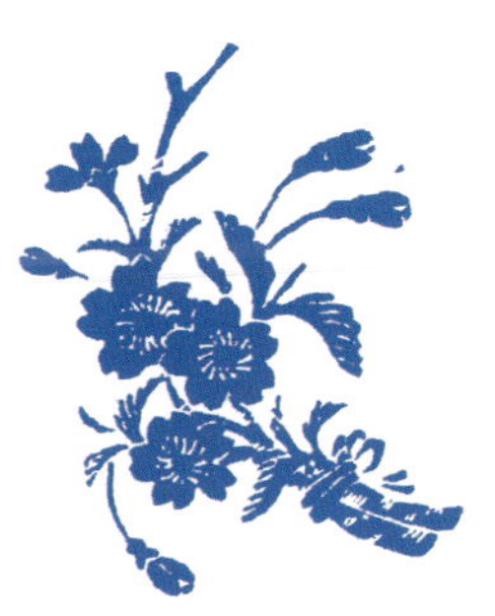

A LOTHIAN BOOK

Contents

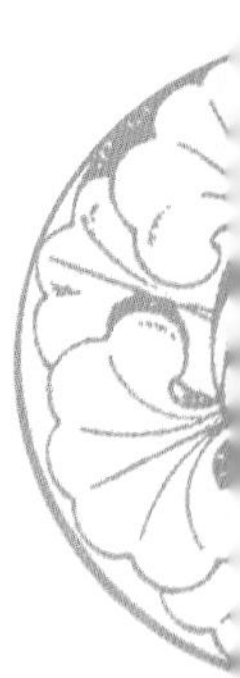

Contents

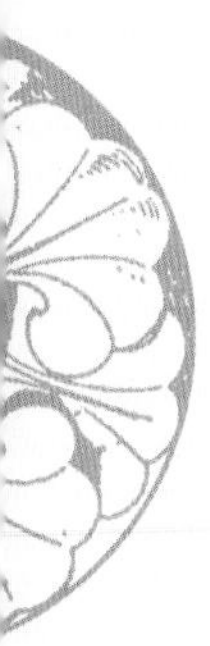

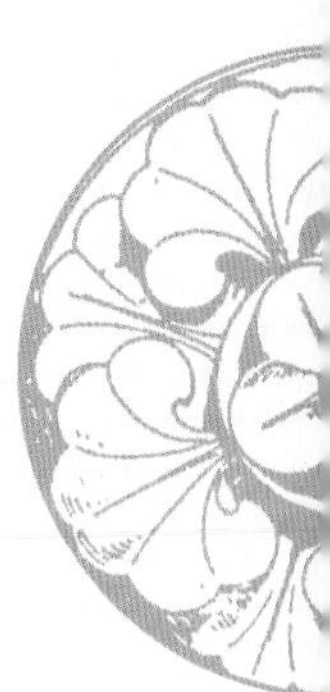

Contents

Introduction

The familiar land we call Australia was not always regarded as welcoming by white settlers: John White, who was a surgeon on the First Fleet, described New South Wales as 'a country and place so forbidding and so hateful as only to merit execration and curses' and Judge Barron Field, author of the first book of Australian verse, formed the opinion that 'No tree...can be beautiful that is not deciduous'. However the rich tradition of landscape painting in Australia over two centuries has seen a profound modification of this view and great masterpieces have been produced as part of our ever-developing cultural heritage—in colonial times, during the period of the Heidelberg Impressionists and more recently with the advent of Modernism and contemporary approaches to the landscape.

Some of the first artists recording visual impressions of Australia took the view that their main role was simply to document the natural terrain, the indigenous peoples, and the flora and the fauna. John Lewin's painting *Two Kangaroos in the Landscape*, which is reproduced here, was intended primarily as an informative work and derives from a series of drawings produced by George Evans during John Oxley's second inland expedition of 1818. John Glover's early Tasmanian painting, on the other hand, combines natural 'data' with 'arcadian' fantasy and reflects the artist's love of plants and vegetation—he was passionate about pastoral landscape and depicted the snow gums and manna gums on the hillside in a naturalistic manner, even if other aspects of the work are reminiscent of a traditional English garden.

While Glover was producing paintings that would be exhibited in London and even sold to the King of France, in due course a style of landscape painting emerged in Australia which was intended primarily for an Australian audience. Conrad Martens led a precarious existence for much of his life in Australia and had to work as a librarian to finance his creativity, but he nevertheless derived most of his income as an artist from local patrons and was therefore instrumental in helping develop an approach to art that was truly Australian.

The artists of the Heidelberg School in Victoria were somewhat more fortunate than Martens in terms of their artistic and financial support. The development of this distinctive, impressionistic approach to painting was made possible in part by the fact that Australian art could be supported by the new-found wealth in such cities as Melbourne, Ballarat, Bendigo and Sydney following the discovery of gold and the development of mining. The

Heidelberg artists extolled the virtues of rural life, appealing to wealthy patrons in the urban areas of Australia who were now interested in the emergent Australian 'mythology' associated with white settlement and 'heritage'. Artists like Roberts and Streeton painted landscapes that emphasised the wholesome and positive qualities of the Australian landscape and David Davies produced his fine nocturnal vistas which evoked an exquisite sense of romantic mystery.

More recently, contemporary artists like John Olsen have been willing to draw our attention to the arid and desolate beauty of Australia—his remarkable painting of Lake Eyre during a time of drought is especially impressive because it is an aerial vista : it summoned for the artist thoughts of 'the void'.

Nevertheless, there is still a sense of the romantic in contemporary approaches to the landscape. Basil Hadley's *Into a Green Experience* and Alasdair McGregor's recent depictions of the outback are both representative examples of this style, and remind us that most Australians seem to have a deep-felt need to respond positively and warmly to what is, for the most part, a harsh and arid environment. This may not be bad thing. We all like to think of our natural landscape as being essentially welcoming, and most of our landscape painters during the last 200 years have tried to capture this quality in their art.

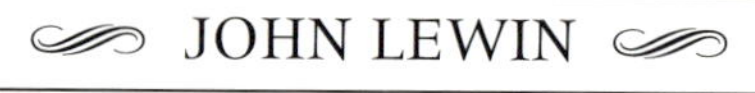

JOHN LEWIN

(1770—1819)

J.W.Lewin 1770-1819
Two Kangaroos in a Landscape 1819
Watercolour 39.5 x 56.5 cm
Rex Nan Kivell Collection
National Library of Australia

Born in London in 1770, John Lewin trained as a botanical artist then came to Sydney as a free settler in 1800, thus earning the right to be known as the first free-born Australian artist. His aim was to make an accurate record of the flora and fauna of the colony and to publish the work in London and pay his return fare with the profits from the sale of the book. Lewin settled in Parramatta to be close to the bush where he could observe and make detailed drawings of the plants and animals and his book duly appeared, in two volumes. Unfortunately, despite the competence and accuracy of the work, the book did not sell well as it seemed the British public was no longer interested in such things.

Lewin accompanied Governor Macquarie on his first official tour across the Blue Mountains in 1815 but he is best remembered for his large, highly finished watercolours of birds and animals which were done under commission for the governors of the colony and for wealthy merchants. He painted the coats of the animals with masses of short brush strokes in several layers of graded tones, thus giving a slightly three dimensional effect. This technique was used in the most famous of his works *Two Kangaroos in a Landscape* (1819), which was painted shortly before his death.

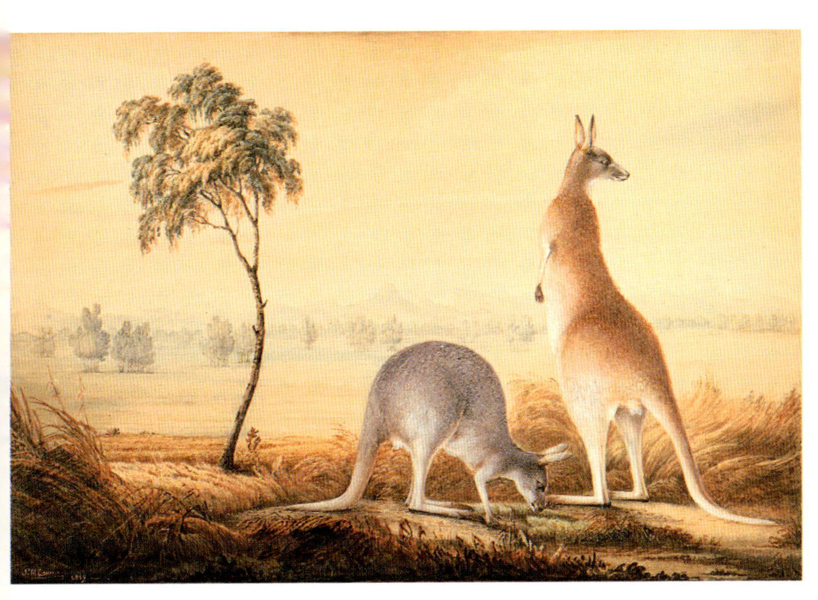

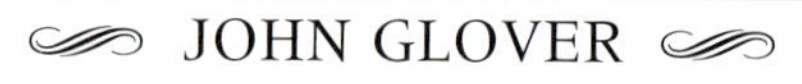

(1767—1849)

John Glover
Australia 1767-1849
A View of the Artist's House and Garden in Mills Plains,
Van Diemen's Land 1834-35
76.4 x 114.4 cm
Art Gallery of South Australia, Adelaide
Morgan Thomas Bequest Fund 1951

A successful English landscape artist and teacher, Glover was at one time so popular he was considered a rival to Turner. He travelled in the English Lake District, France, Germany and Italy and in 1831, just after his sixty fourth birthday, he arrived in Tasmania to join his three sons who were farming near Hobart. A wealthy man, he received a grant of land at Mills Plains where he established an English country garden.

Even the name 'Patterdale' was taken from a village in the Lake District and the garden was planted with introduced flowers which Glover had chosen to complete his 'Arcadia'.

Glover was the first resident professional artist to attempt to paint the Australian bush. He made numerous pictures of his own farm and of the surrounding districts of Mount Olympus and Lake St Clair. *A View of the Artist's House and Garden in Mills Plains, Van Diemen's Land c.1835* is typical of his work.

Unlike many artists at the time, Glover did recognise the difference between Australian and European vegetation and tried to depict these accurately. One of his earliest observations about the trees in this new land was that no matter how numerous they were, it was always possible to see the space between them and that unlike European trees, they rarely blocked the whole horizon.

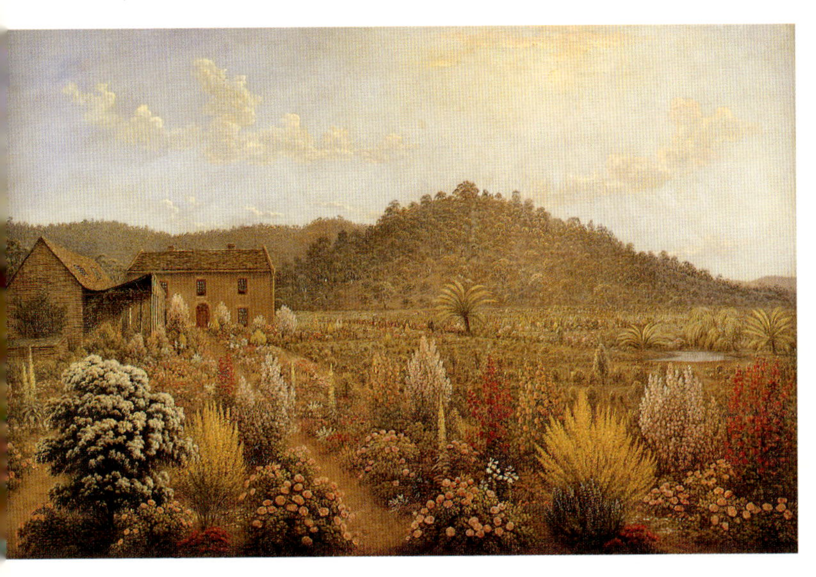

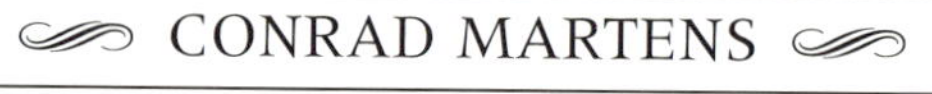

CONRAD MARTENS

(1801—1878)

Conrad Martens
Australia 1801-1878
Wiseman's Ferry in 1838
oil on canvas 47 x 66 cm
Art Gallery of New South Wales
Bequest of A. A. Vickery 1942

Martens was the son of an Austrian diplomat who had settled in London. He studied landscape painting under the English watercolourist Copley Fielding who taught him how to catch the atmosphere of filtered sunlight after rain. He was also influenced by Turner and, like him, believed that light was the most dramatic element in nature.

In 1832 Martens joined the crew of a ship as topographical artist and recorder and later, in Rio de Janeiro, transferred to the *Beagle* where he worked with Charles Darwin and eventually arrived in Sydney via Tahiti in 1835. Martens spent the rest of his life in Sydney painting many scenes of the harbour and the surrounding countryside. He was the first artist to deliberately set out to develop and promote art in the colony which he constantly deplored as a 'cultural backwater'. Martens gave lectures and demonstrations on watercolour painting in an attempt to 'improve' society and his efforts were well received. A married man with children, Martens managed to support his family by painting and teaching, quite a remarkable achievement in the early days of the colony. Martens' romantic style and his tendency to paint landscapes dominated by the sky or weather are well illustrated in his work *Wiseman's Ferry*.

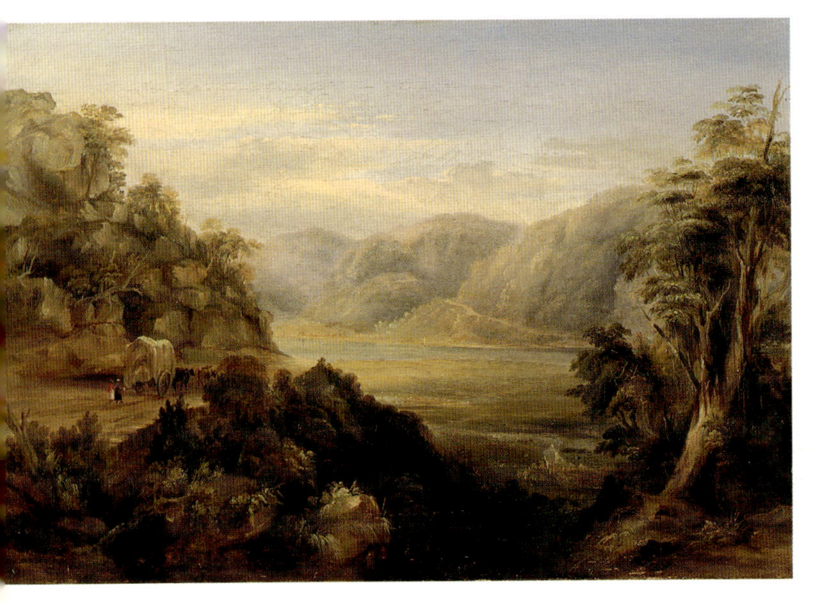

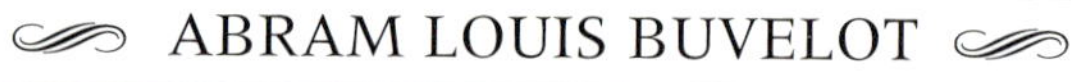

(1814—1888)

Abram Louis Buvelot 1814-1888 Australian
Winter Morning near Heidelberg 1866
oil on canvas
76.2 x 118.2 cm
National Gallery of Victoria
Purchased 1869

Often described as the father of Australian landscape painting, Swiss-born Louis Buvelot was already an established artist who had spent nearly twenty years in Brazil before he migrated to Australia in 1865 hoping that the climate here would improve his health. He was familiar with the French technique of 'plein-air' painting and was the first European to work outside, directly from nature, and to analyse the colours of the Australian landscape and attempt to reproduce the quality of its light. Buvelot spoke little English and on his arrival in Melbourne he set himself up as a photographer while his wife gave French lessons. By 1869 he was considered the colony's leading landscape artist and had gained the admiration of Julian Ashton and a group of young art students such as Tom Roberts, Arthur Streeton and Frederick McCubbin who would later go on to form the 'Heidelberg School'.

Buvelot painted peaceful rural scenes which were often reminiscent of Europe. He spent many hours contemplating a scene before attempting to paint it and was especially attracted to the soft colours of early morning or late afternoon. *Winter Morning near Heidelberg* 1866 is a typical example of his work as is *Summer Afternoon, Templestowe*, painted in the same year.

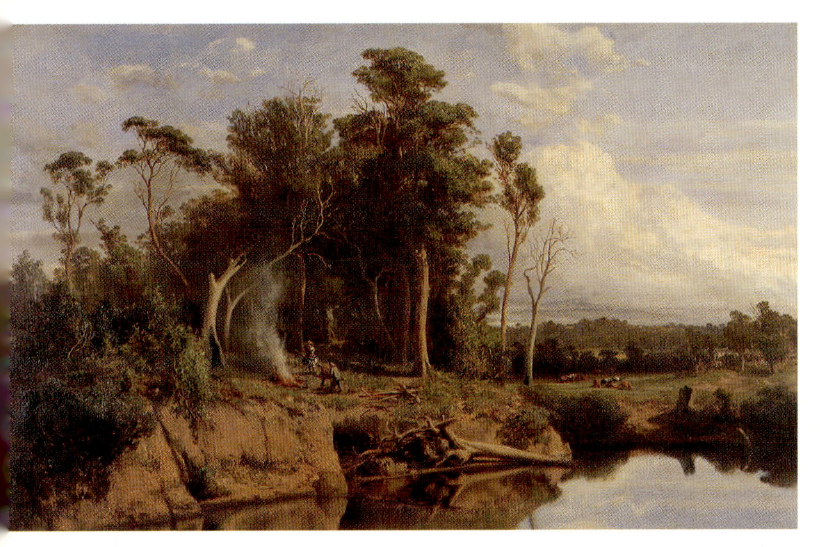

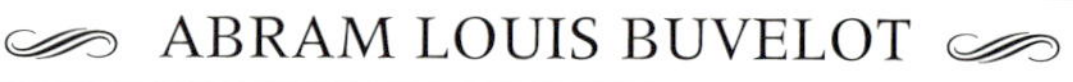

ABRAM LOUIS BUVELOT

(1814—1888)

Abram Louis Buvelot 1814-1888 Australian
Summer Afternoon, Templestowe 1866
oil on canvas
76.2 x 118.8 cm
National Gallery of Victoria
Purchased 1989

Often described as the father of Australian landscape painting, Swiss-born Louis Buvelot was already an established artist who had spent nearly twenty years in Brazil before he migrated to Australia in 1865 hoping that the climate here would improve his health. He was familiar with the French technique of 'plein-air' painting and was the first European to work outside, directly from nature, and to analyse the colours of the Australian landscape and attempt to reproduce the quality of its light. Buvelot spoke little English and on his arrival in Melbourne he set himself up as a photographer while his wife gave French lessons. By 1869 he was considered the colony's leading landscape artist and had gained the admiration of Julian Ashton and a group of young art students such as Tom Roberts, Arthur Streeton and Frederick McCubbin who would later go on to form the 'Heidelberg School'.

Buvelot painted peaceful rural scenes which were often reminiscent of Europe. He spent many hours contemplating a scene before attempting to paint it and was especially attracted to the soft colours of early morning or late afternoon. *Winter Morning near Heidelberg* 1866 is a typical example of his work as is *Summer Afternoon, Templestowe*, painted in the same year.

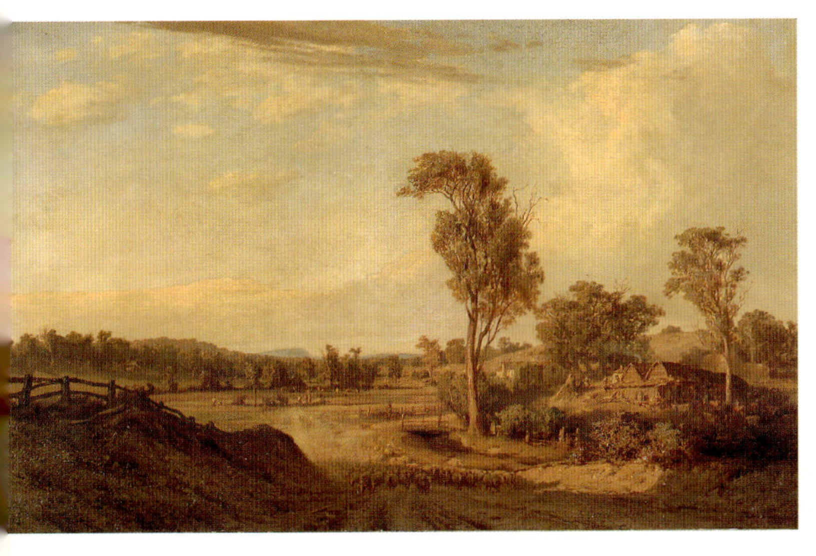

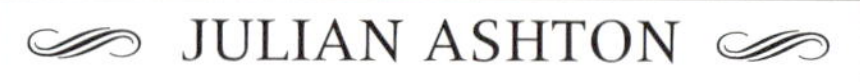

(1851—1942)

Julian Ashton 1851-1942 Australian
The Corner of the Paddock 1888
watercolour
40.5 x 58.8 cm
National Gallery of Victoria
Purchased with the assistance of a special grant from the Government of Victoria, 1979

Better known today as a teacher than as an artist, Julian Ashton was born in England and worked there first as a draughtsman then as an illustrator. He came to Melbourne in 1878 to take up a position with the Australian *Illustrated News* and travelled the country widely as a staff artist for this and other similar journals. Ashton was a friend of Louis Buvelot and became a central figure in the 'plein air' painting group. In 1885 he was appointed director of classes run by the Art Society of New South Wales and later became a trustee of the Art Gallery of New South Wales where he actively worked to increase the number of Australian paintings. Ashton believed artists should work from first-hand experience, from familiar scenes and landscape which 'charms the eye'. His work *The Corner of the Paddock 1888*, painted at Richmond in NSW is a good example of these principles at work.

In 1896 Ashton established his own 'Academy Julian' which became Sydney's leading art school and was to influence such students as Sydney Ure Smith, Elioth Gruner and later William Dobell and John Passmore. He was awarded the first Society of Artists medal in 1924 and the C. B. E. for services to art in 1930.

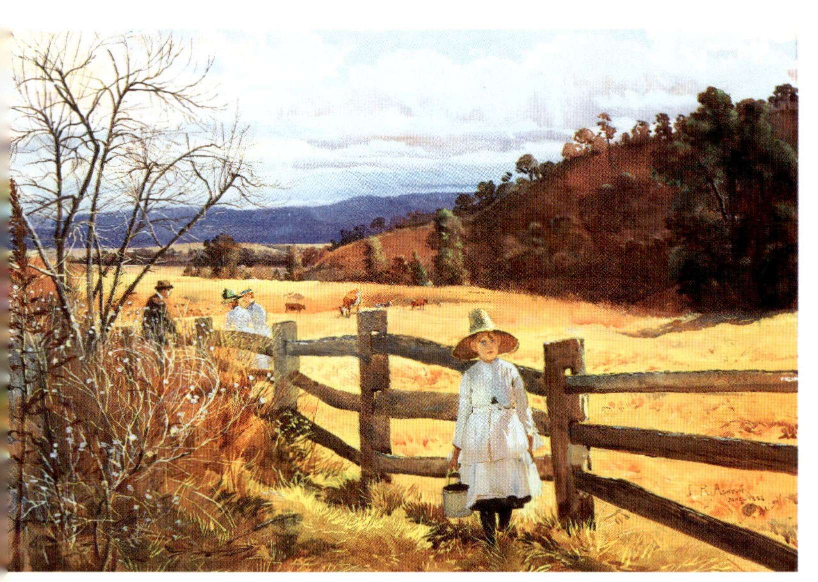

CHARLES EDWARD CONDER

(1868—1909)

Charles Conder 1868-1909 Australian
Yarding Sheep 1890
oil on canvas
36.2 x 55.8 cm
National Gallery of Victoria
Bequeathed by Mrs E.E. Leep, 1944

Although Conder is one of the best known of early Australian painters, he actually spent only seven years in the country. His father, an English railway engineer, disapproved of his son's interest in art and sent the sixteen year old boy out to New South Wales to be apprenticed to his uncle who was a surveyor with the Lands Department. However the ambitions of the young Charles were not so easily thwarted and with the support of his uncle, he enrolled in evening art classes and in 1886 was employed as an illustrator on the *Illustrated Sydney News*. Conder met Julian Ashton and became friendly with Tom Roberts who worked with him at Coogee and Bondi and later invited him to join the Box Hill camp. *Yarding Sheep 1890* shows the influence of Conder's time spent in the outback on surveyors' camps. The washed out colours convey the shimmering heat and dust-laden atmosphere so characteristic of the Australian summer.

In 1990 when he was twenty-two he returned to Europe where he became involved in the bohemian art scene of Paris and led a dissipated life which had serious effects on his health. He continued to paint and make lithographs in Paris and London where he knew Aubrey Beardsley and Oscar Wilde.

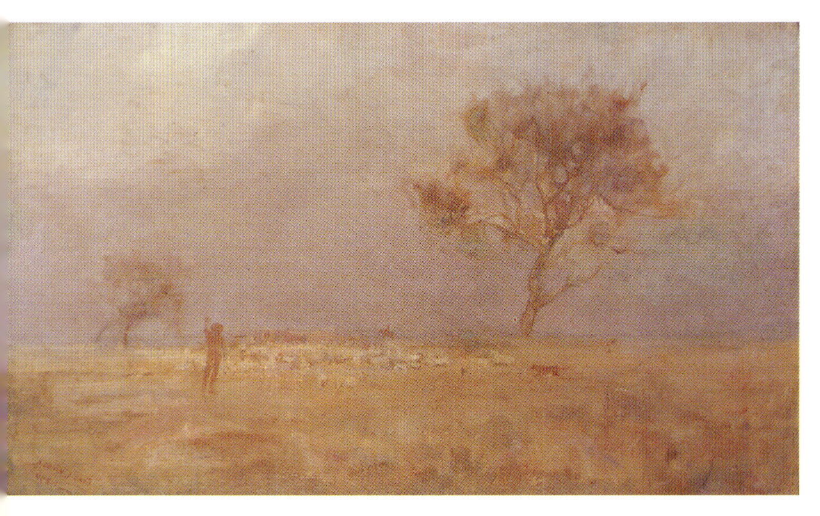

(SIR) ARTHUR ERNEST STREETON

(1867—1943)

Arthur Streeton 1867-1943 Australian
The Purple Noon's Transparent Might 1896
oil on canvas
121.8 x 122.0 cm
National Gallery of Victoria
Purchased 1896

Born near Geelong in Victoria, Streeton (nicknamed 'Smike' because of his slight build), was the fourth child of a schoolteacher. He left school to work in the warehouse of an importer of rum and spirits but soon took up night classes at art school and began to make regular 'plein air' painting excursions out into the countryside with other young artists such as Tom Roberts, Charles Conder and Frederick McCubbin. The term 'Heidelberg school', used to describe these artists, was actually coined in a review of an exhibition of Streeton's work. Streeton loved the vastness and depth of the Australian landscape which he described as the land of the 'blue and gold' and his feelings of awe and wonder at the light and colour of the countryside led him to bestow quite romantic titles on many of his paintings. *The Purple Noon's Transparent Might (1896*) is a view of the Hawkesbury River, west of Sydney with the Blue Mountains in the background.

Streeton, like many of his contemporaries, left Australia for Europe where he travelled widely and had several successful exhibitions. When he returned permanently in 1929 he became art critic for *The Argus* and did much to revive public interest in the Heidelberg school. He was knighted in 1937.

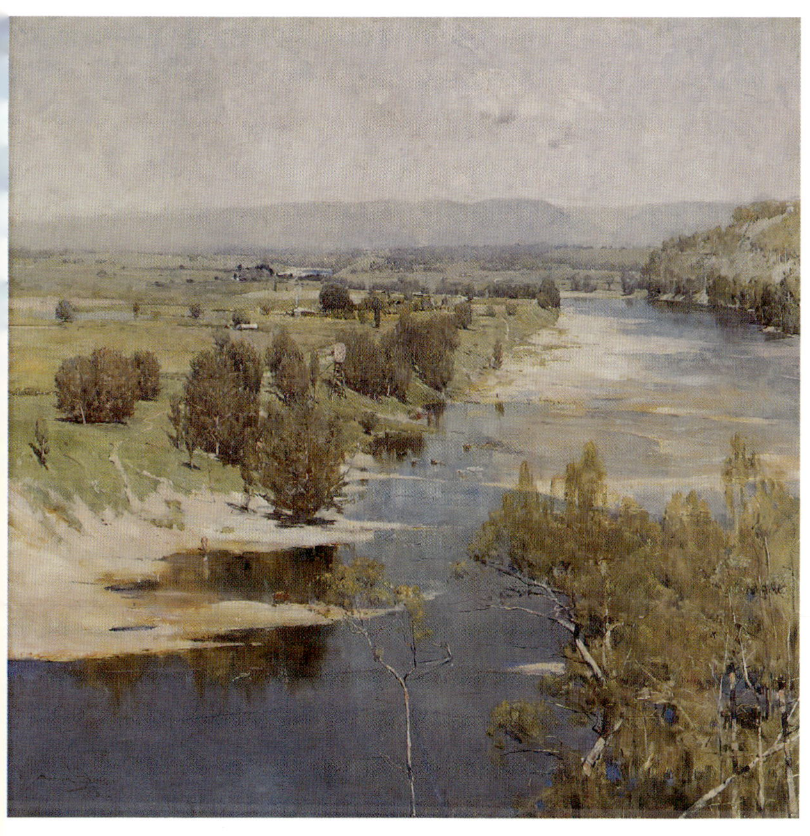

TOM (THOMAS WILLIAM) ROBERTS

(1856—1931)

Tom Roberts
Mosman's Bay 1894
Gift of Howard Hinton, 1933
the Howard Hinton Collection
New England Regional Art Museum
Armidale NSW

Born in Dorchester, England, Roberts, emigrated to Melbourne when he was a young teenager. Always interested in art he studied at the Gallery school under Louis Buvelot where he became a student of some influence, constantly advocating adventurous, new ideas such as the introduction of life drawing classes. He travelled to Spain on a walking tour where he met two other young artists who had studied plein air painting in Paris. Roberts recognised the similarities of this technique to the work Buvelot had been doing in Australia and when he returned in 1885 he was inspired to challenge the conservative establishment. Together with Frederick McCubbin he camped at Box Hill outside Melbourne to paint sunlit and twilight landscapes rapidly, with a broad brush and paying attention to the light and colour of entire views rather than to detail. Roberts led several expeditions and became a leader of the painters known as the Heidelberg school. In 1888 he travelled to Sydney and by 1891 Roberts and Arthur Streeton were living at Curlew Camp on Little Sirius Cove near Mosman, Sydney. This camp was a semi-permanent institution inhabited by artists and other bohemian characters and it was from here that Roberts painted *Mosman's Bay* in 1894, a work which shows influences of his friends Streeton and Conder. Roberts also became a fashionable portrait artist.

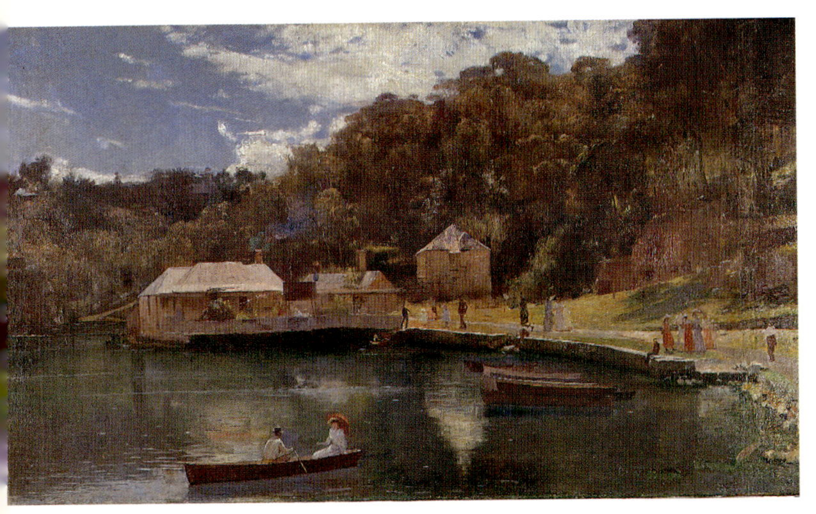

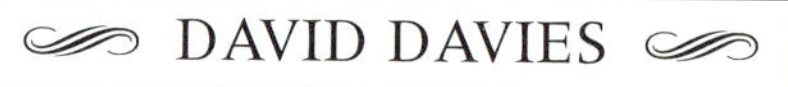

DAVID DAVIES

(1864—1939)

David Davies 1864-1939 Australian
Evening, Templestowe 1897
oil on canvas
45.0 x 56.0 cm
National Gallery of Victoria
Purchased with the assistance of a special grant from the Government of Victoria, 1979

The son of a gold miner in Ballarat, Davies began his art studies at the local school of design before moving to Melbourne where in 1888 he won the student landscape prize for his work *The Hot Day*. Two years later he left for Europe where he studied in Paris and joined a colony of plein air artists in Cornwall and studied the work of the English Impressionists, particularly Whistler. He returned to Australia in 1893 to live at Templestowe in Victoria where he painted his famous 'Moonrise' series. While many Heidelberg painters were interested in the harsh sunlight of the Australian landscape, Davies preferred to paint the qualities of the landscape at dusk, the mysterious dark shadows and the romantic reflections of the moon, and was concerned with exploring the soul or spirit of the land. Davies was a part of the family who owned the Eaglemont Estate where so many of the Heidelberg painters gathered to work. In 1897 he and his wife returned to Europe where he held several exhibitions and remained for most of the rest of his life, holding only one major exhibition in Australia in 1926.

Evening, Templestowe, 1897, is typical of the studies of the light of early evening scenes which Davies produced in the 1890s.

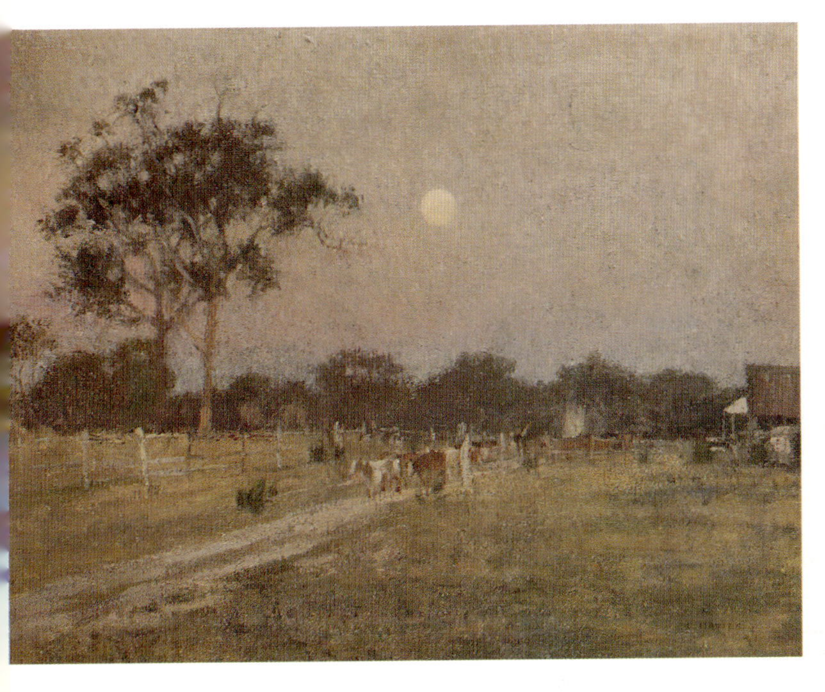

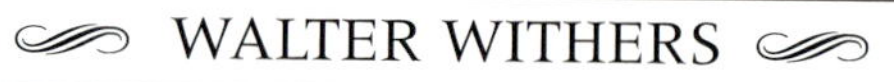

WALTER WITHERS

(1854—1914)

Walter Withers 1854-1914 Australian
A Bright Winter's Morning 1894
oil on canvas
60.8 x 91.4 cm
National Gallery of Victoria
Bequeathed by Mrs Nina Sheppard 1956

As a young man Withers studied at respected art schools hoping to emulate the career of his grandfather. But his father sent his son to the colonies hoping he would be distracted from his artistic inclinations. In 1882 Withers packed a swag and spent eighteen months working on the land and when he returned to Melbourne he was delighted to be able to sell some of his sketches and to resume his art studies, this time at the National Gallery of Victoria. He returned briefly to England where he married, spent some time at the Academie Julian in Paris and then came back to Australia to take up a job as illustrator for *Chronicles of Early Melbourne* by Edmund Finn. During this time he painted at Eaglemont with Tom Roberts, Arthur Streeton and Charles Conder then took over part of 'Charterisville', an old mansion at Heidelberg where he painted while his wife gave music lessons. He also established a city teaching studio at which Norman Lindsay enrolled in one of his plein air classes. *A Bright Winter's Morning,* which he painted in 1894, is typical of the romantic treatment Withers gave to his subjects. Withers was a leading figure in Melbourne's artistic circles and a founding member of the Australian Art Association. Withers was also a trustee of the National Gallery of Victoria.

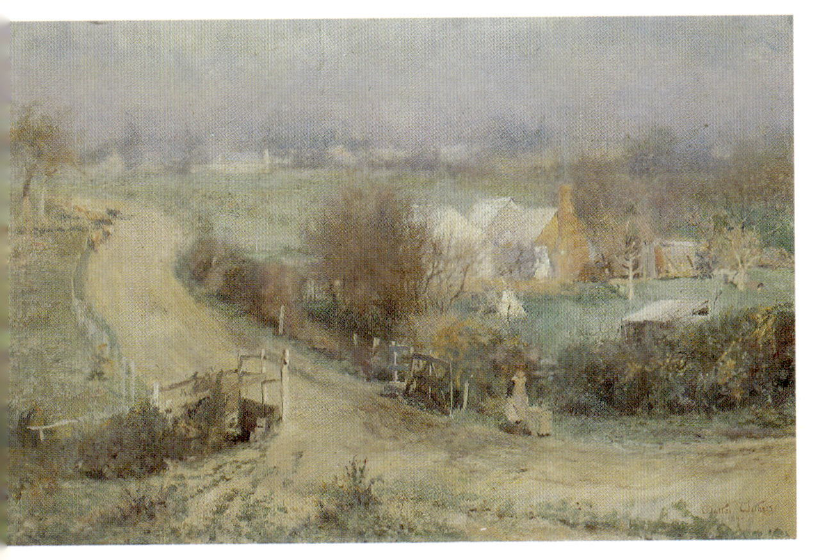

 EMMANUEL PHILLIPS FOX 

(1865—1915)

Emmanuel Phillips Fox 1865-1915 Australian
Moonrise, Heidelberg 1902
oil on canvas
75.8 x 126.5 cm
National Gallery of Victoria
Purchased 1948

The son of a Melbourne photographer, Fox trained at the National Gallery School where he won a prize for landscape painting and qualified as a teacher of drawing. He taught at various schools of design while pursuing his own studies as a painter then in 1887 left for Paris. Here he passed the rigorous entrance exam for the School des Beaux-Arts and won first prize in his class. He joined plein air expeditions to Brittany and Cornwall and visited Madrid before returning to Australia where with Tudor St George Tucker he established the Melbourne Art School which taught plein air and impressionist principles. During his time in Europe Phillips Fox had painted many moonlight scenes; *Moonrise, Heidelberg (1900)* painted near Melbourne, was the first of several versions of the same picture in which he continued to develop this interest.He won a joint commission to produce Australian historical paintings for the National Gallery of Victoria and in order to fulfil the extraordinary terms of the bequest he left for England to produce *The Landing of Captain Cook at Botany Bay*, one of his most famous paintings.

In 1904 he became the first Australian-born artist to receive a gold medal from the new Salon des Artistes Francais. In 1913 he returned to Australia where he was much admired by young artists for the bright colours of his French-influenced paintings.

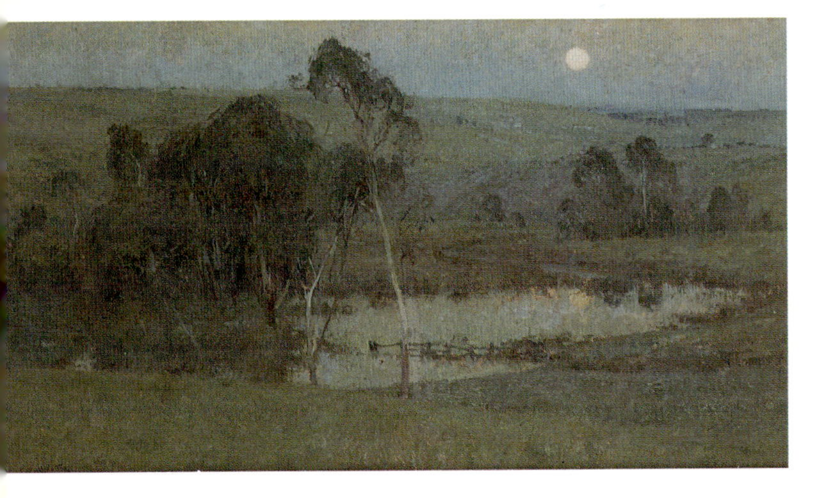

FREDERICK McCUBBIN

(1855—1917)

Frederick McCubbin 1855-1917 Australian
A Winter Evening 1897
oil on canvas
123.0 x 153.0 cm
National Gallery of Victoria
Purchased 1900

The son of a Melbourne baker, McCubbin left school at 14 but even at this age showed a keen interest in drawing and enrolled himself in a weekly class at the Artisan's School of Design. He was one of the few young Australian artists of this time whose training took place entirely in this country, in his case mostly at Melbourne's National Gallery School. Many of his earlier paintings have strong social themes and are influenced by the early plein air painters such as Buvelot. Though somewhat limited in his activities by his seven small children, McCubbin regularly associated with Tom Roberts and Louis Abrahams (McCubbin's first child was named Louis) and was an active member of the Australian Artists' Association and a popular drawing master at the Gallery School. A review of McCubbin's exhibition which included *A Winter Evening* 1897 suggested they were painted by an artist 'happy in his life and surroundings, fully alive and keenly perceptible of the subtle changes of sunshine and air'. McCubbin made his only trip to Europe in 1907 when he was over fifty. He returned feeling overwhelmed by the masterpieces he had seen and for the last ten years of his life painted only small landscapes in the style of Turner and the mainstream Impressionists.

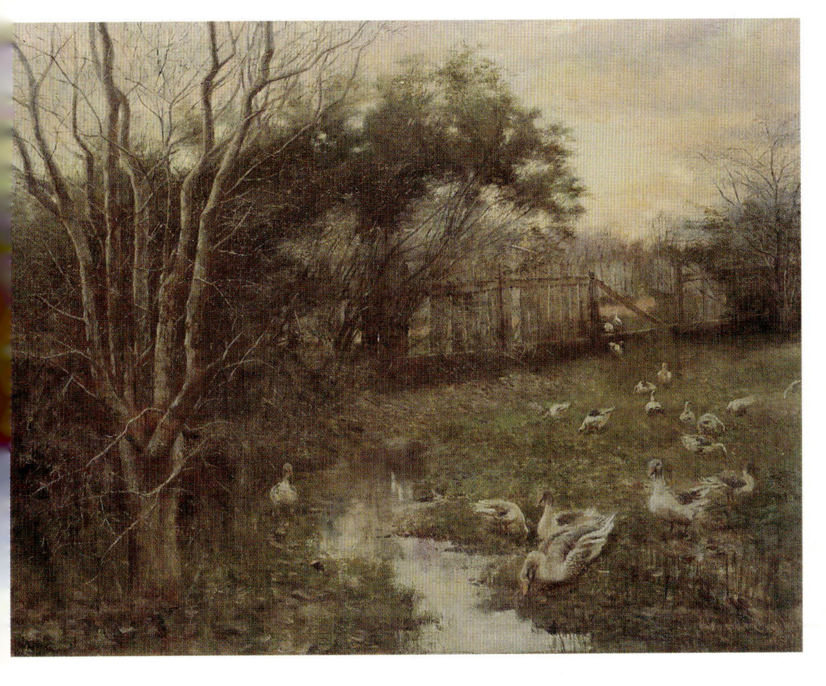

ELIOTH GRUNER

(1882—1939)

Elioth Gruner
Australian 1882-1939
Valley of the Tweed 1921
oil on canvas 142.2 x 172.7 cm
Art Gallery of New South Wales
Commissioned by the Trustees 1919

Born in New Zealand to an Irish mother and a Norwegian father, Elioth Gruner came to Australia when he was only a year old. He left school at fourteen to work in a store during the day and study in the evenings at Julian Ashton's School of Art where he later became a teacher. His gentle landscapes were influenced by the now popular plein air methods and the French classical landscape painter, Corot, and were concerned with depicting the atmospheric effects of early morning light and mist. Gruner camped in the bush for long periods and rose at dawn to attempt to capture the atmosphere. In 1923 he travelled to London to manage an Australian Exhibition at the Royal Academy which included eight of his own works. He remained in Europe to study for two years. When he returned his work became more structured with a greater emphasis on formal elements. Some critics maintained that Gruner's work broke no new ground and he merely did well what others had done before; nevertheless his work was popular and he was awarded the Wynne Prize seven times. His fourth Wynne Prize was awarded for what is regarded as one of his best works, *Valley of the Tweed(1921)*. Despite his popular success, Gruner was a lonely and unhappy man.

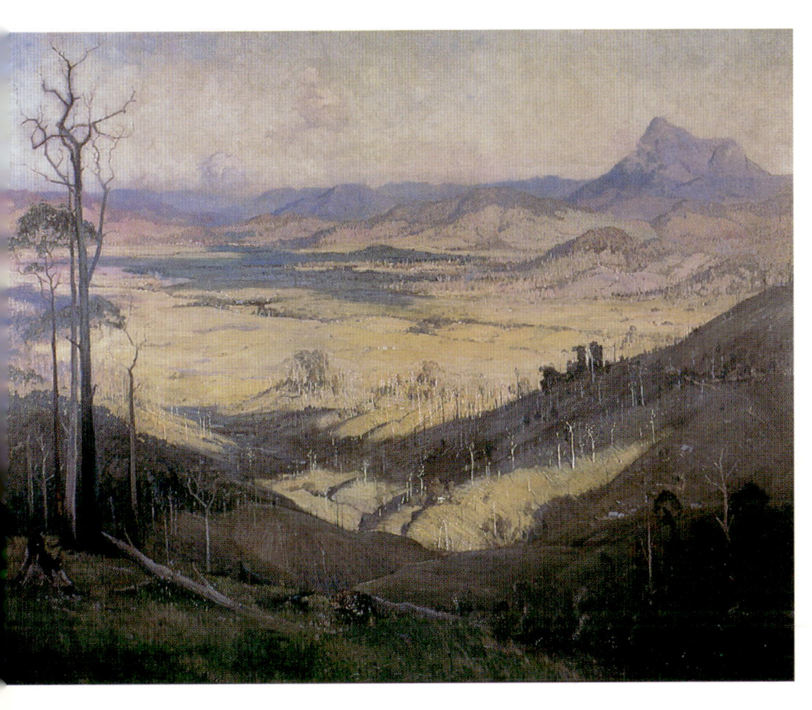

MARGARET PRESTON

(1875—1963)

Margaret Preston
Australian 1875-1963
Aboriginal Landscape 1941
oil on canvas 40.0 x 52.0 cm
Art Gallery of South Australia, Adelaide
D. & J.T. Mortlock Bequest Fund 1982

Margaret Rose McPherson, generally known as Rose, was a confident, assertive child who is said to have decided on a career as an artist when, as a twelve year old student at Fort Street School, she visited the Art Gallery of New South Wales and imagined herself gaining public admiration as one of the students working in the gallery and enjoying the smell of the floor polish. She began art classes soon after and with energy and enthusiasm began her training towards a very successful career.

As a young woman she made two lengthy visits to Europe where she studied, painted and visited a wide range of contemporary galleries. Returning to Australia after World War 1 she met and married a fellow Australian, William Preston, who provided both affection and financial security.

Margaret Preston's Aboriginal style paintings are characteristic of the later period of her work. She had a strong interest in promoting the indigenous art of Australia for nationalistic reasons and made several long and arduous trips to remote areas to study Aboriginal art. Her *Aboriginal Landscape (1941)* is a good example of her work in this style. Realising there was a need to educate the public at the time it was produced, she wrote 'Aboriginal Art represents not the object alone from which it was drawn, but the essential truths which may or may not be visible to the human eye.'

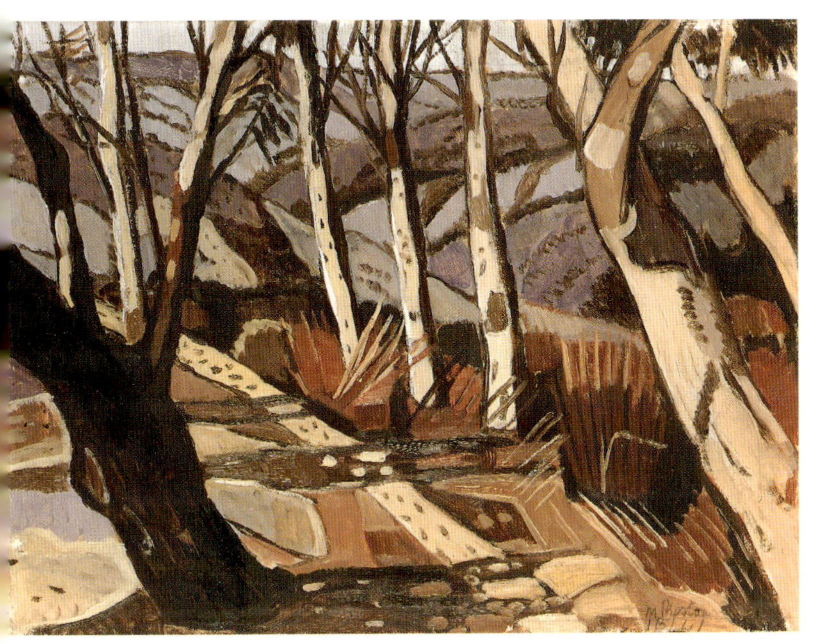

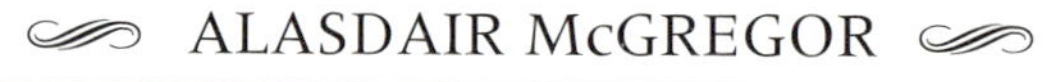

ALASDAIR McGREGOR

(1954—)

Alasdair McGregor
Through Canegrass and Elephant Ear Wattle 1992
oil on canvas
137 x 122 cm
Courtesy of Painters Gallery Australia, Sydney

After graduating with honours in an Architecture degree from the University of New South Wales, Sydney-born Alasdair McGregor divided his time between working in the profession for which he had been trained and painting, an area in which he was self taught. He made three visits to the Antarctic region during the 1980s as well as several trips into remote areas of Australia. These expeditions have been the source of inspiration for much of his work and since 1987 he has devoted himself almost exclusively to painting.

McGregor has held several solo exhibitions in the major cities of Australia and has produced commissioned work for several organisations such as Australia Post, the Australian Antarctic Division and the Hilton Hotel, Brisbane. His work is represented in both private and corporate collections in Australia and overseas. In 1990 he was invited to take part in the Kakadu 'Artist's Camp' and he has recently produced a book on the natural history of the Kimberley region.

McGregor's work is always derived from wilderness landscape and natural history. He aims to achieve a static quality in his work and, through a preoccupation with details of colour and form, to imbue his pictures with an awareness of the Australian environment.

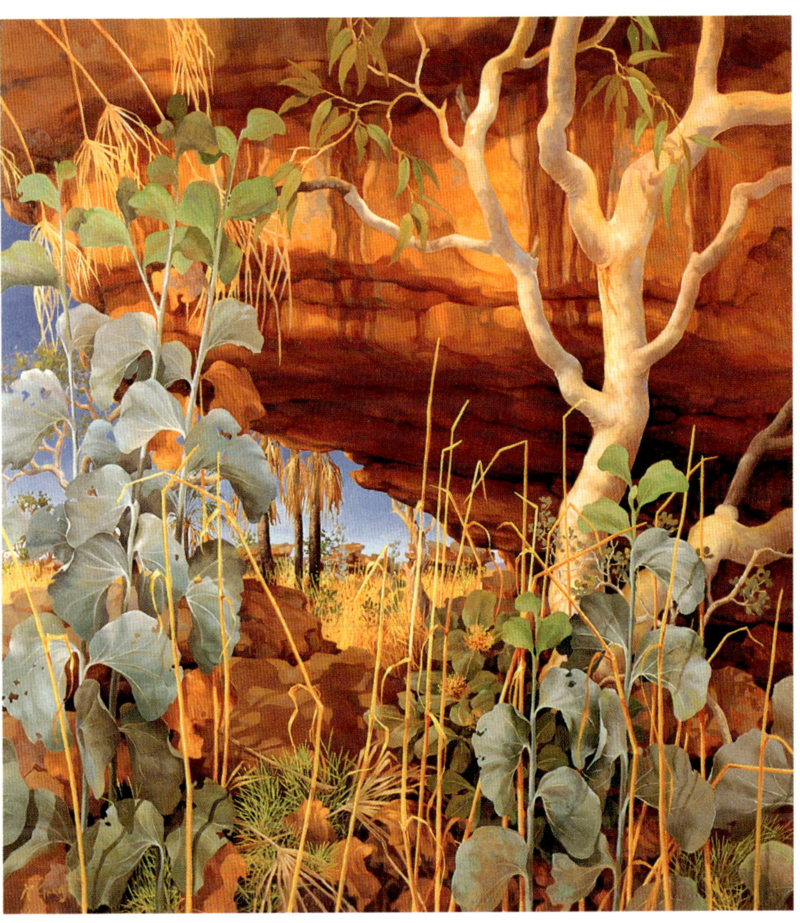

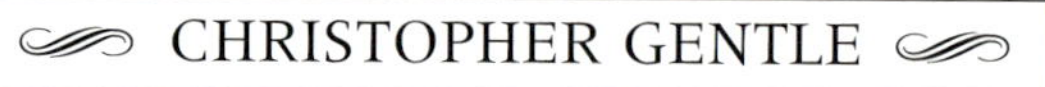

CHRISTOPHER GENTLE

(1939—)

Christopher Gentle 1939 -
Late Afternoon in the Kimberley 1990
oil on canvas 76 x 91 cm
Courtesy of the painter

Born in England, Gentle studied painting, drawing, sculpture and lithography at the West Sussex College of Art. He spent two years travelling through the West Indies, USA, Canada and New Zealand before settling in Australia in 1967. After almost a decade of experience as Director of the Ivan Dougherty Gallery, Sydney, he took up a position as Senior Lecturer at the City Art Institute.

Gentle's work is represented in several major galleries in Australia as well as in corporate and private collections both here and overseas.

In 1983 Gentle spent three months in central Australia drawing, painting and photographing the dramatic landforms and a year later travelled to the Northern Territory to work on commissioned drawings of the landscape. He is particularly interested in the processes of Nature—of growth, decay and regeneration and the evidence of Nature at work in the landscape. In many of his works he has used the landscape as a metaphor for his own experiences and his accumulated understanding of the human condition.

Late Afternoon in the Kimberley is a good example of his work.

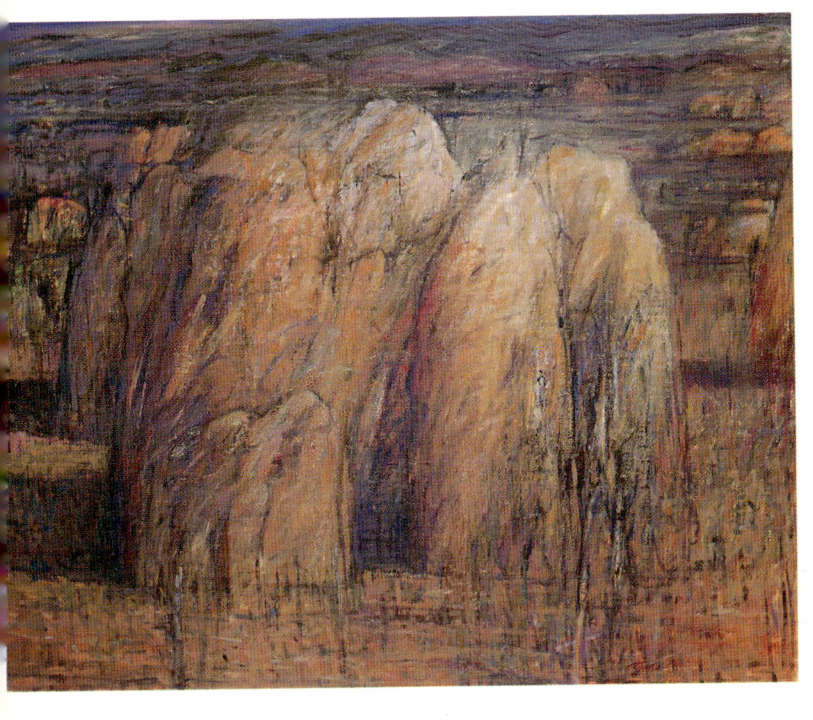

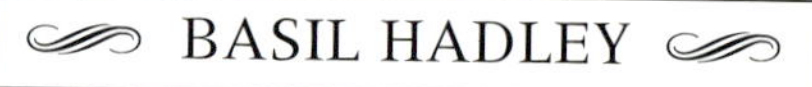

BASIL HADLEY

(1940—)

Basil Hadley 1940-
Into a Green Experience 1989
oil on canvas 92 x 102 cm
Private Collection

Hadley was born in London and, after studying at the Ealing College of Art, had his first one man exhibition in London when he was only 21. In 1964 he emigrated to Australia where he studied for a short time at the Prahran College of Advanced Education but since then his development as an artist has been largely self-directed. Hadley has had numerous exhibitions both in the capital cities of Australia and in regional capitals and his work has been shown in Sweden, Japan, Singapore and Korea. He has won numerous regional art prizes and has been commissioned by a number of corporations, including the Sheraton Hotels in Alice Springs and Darwin.

Hadley has done a number of landscape paintings particularly his Kakadu series from 1988-90 which includes *Into a Green Experience (1989)*. He worked as artist-in-residence in Kakadu with the Northern Territories Museums and Art Galleries and made several low level flights on mail runs to isolated homesteads. Observation from this angle led to the production of a series of paintings often scattered with delicate stick-like trees or grass painted with startling clarity. Hadley himself has remarked that the vast emptiness of the Australian landscape with its lack of human presence 'tends to put me in my place and give me a sense of truth and timelessness'.

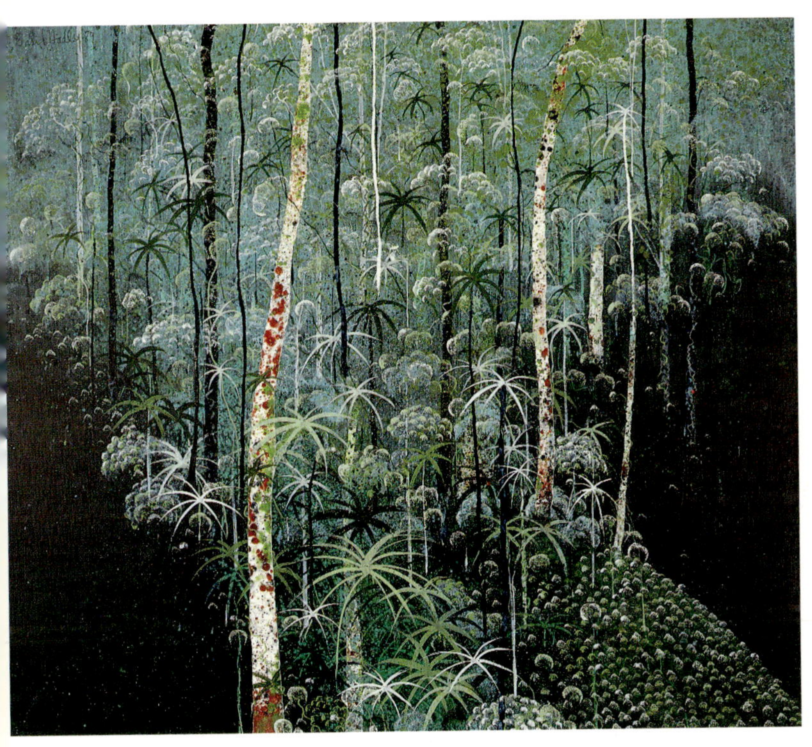

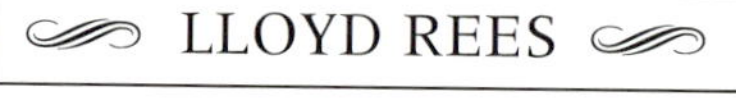

LLOYD REES

(1895—1988)

Lloyd Rees
Australia 1895-1988
The Road to Berry 1947
oil on canvas on paperboard
34.6 x 42.2 cm
Art Gallery of New South Wales
Purchased 1947

Born in Brisbane of Welsh and French descent, Lloyd Rees felt a life-long affinity with European culture. Lloyd showed artistic ability from a very early age but nevertheless at the age of 16 was put to work as a clerk in an insurance office. A long illness allowed him to escape and he began to attend evening classes where he developed a strong interest in architecture. At 22 he came to Sydney to work as a commercial artist for Sydney Ure Smith, the publisher of *Art in Australia,* and began for the first time to experiment with oil painting. In 1923 he spent a year overseas studying painting in France, Italy and then London before returning to Sydney.

Rees painted a great many landscapes and was particularly attracted to vistas of sweeping hills with a valley in the foreground, as in *The Road to Berry (1947)*. This tiny picture was painted under a copse of trees which appear later in *The Road to the Mountain (1954)*, a larger work which was very much influenced by the earlier one. Painted outside the village hall in Gerringong NSW, this picture (96x116.8cm) was the biggest painting Rees had ever done outdoors and the physical effort of carrying the canvas to the site was considerable so the artist had to be driven to the site and then picked up several hours later.

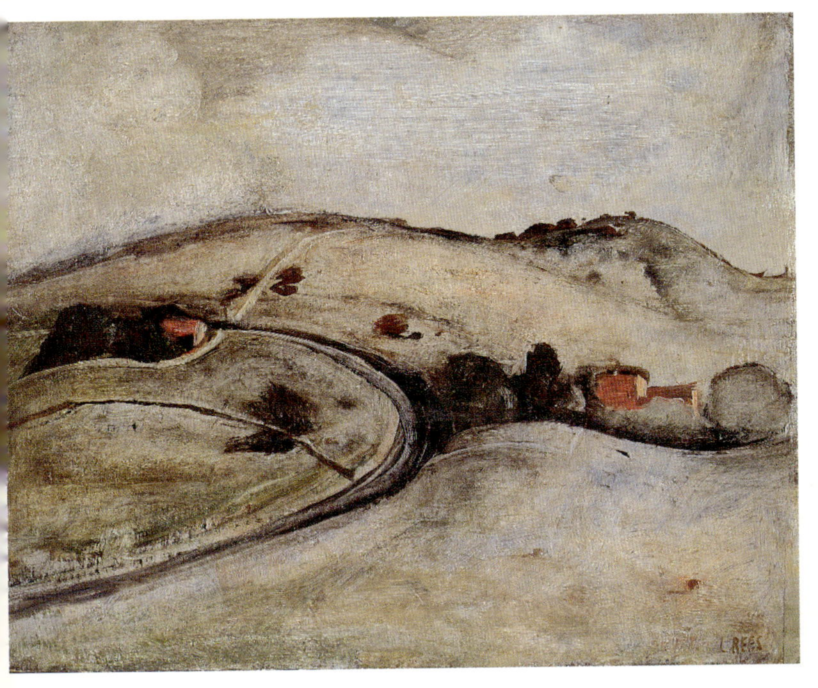
L REES

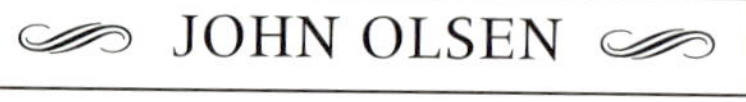

(1928—)

John Olsen 1928 –
Lake Eyre 1975
Oil on canvas 214 x 200cm

Born in Newcastle, Olsen came to Sydney as a small child. He studied with Desiderius Orban and then attended night classes at the Julian Ashton School of Art. In 1956 his works were represented in the controversial group exhibition 'Direction 1'. Not one of these exclusively abstract paintings was sold—they were obviously too far ahead of public taste at the time—and the following year Olsen left for Paris and Spain where he studied and worked for the next three years. On his return to Sydney he established his reputation as one of the most exciting of Australia's modernist painters with his *You Beaut Country* series and in 1972 he was commissioned to paint the *Salute to Five Bells* mural in the Sydney Opera House. He was awarded the Wynne Prize for landscape painting in 1969 and 1985.

During the 1970's Olsen visited Lake Eyre three times with the naturalist Vincent Serventy. On the first visit the lake was flooded and Olsen described standing beside it as like being on the 'edge of the world'. As he camped beside the lake he became absorbed by the tiny details of insects and flowers, then as he flew over the water in a plane he became aware of the relationship of the lake to the broader environs. The painting *Lake Eyre* captures the feeling of spiritual openness that Olsen experienced and also reflects the artist's love of Oriental art.

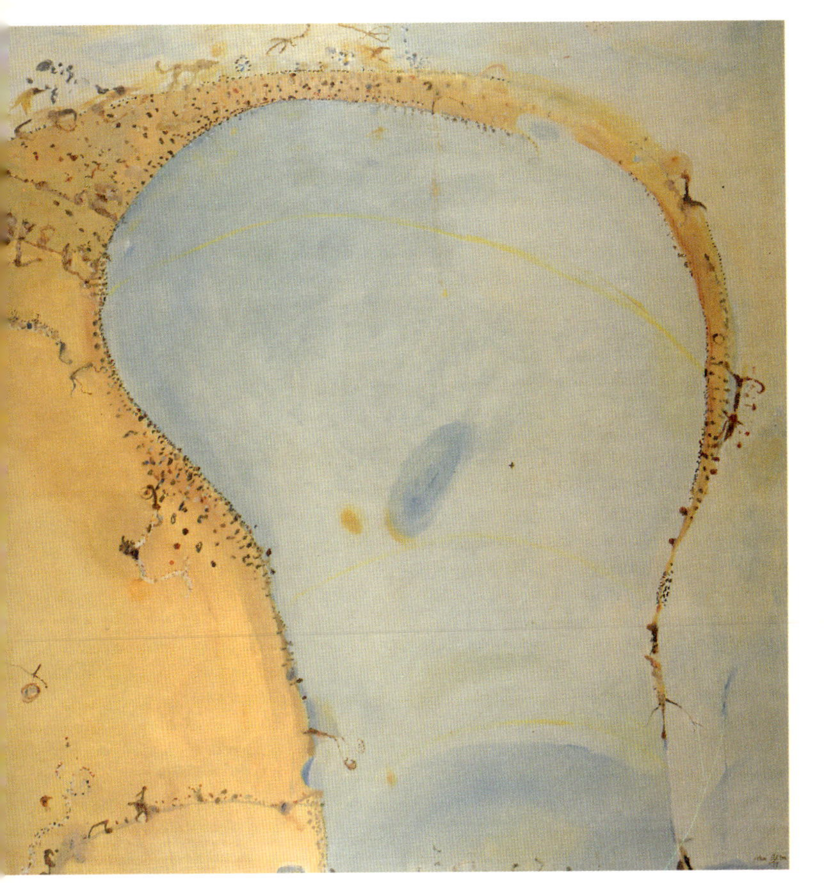

A Lothian Book

Thomas C. Lothian Publishing Company Pty Ltd
11 Munro Street, Port Melbourne, Victoria 3207

First published 1993

National Library of Australia
Cataloguing-in-publication data

Stuart, Elizabeth.
Australian landscapes.

ISBN 0 85091 599 6.

1. Landscape painting – Australia. 2. Landscape painters – Australia. I Title.
(Series : Australian art masters).

759.994

A Sandpiper Press Production

Published in association with Sandpiper Press (NSW) Pty. Ltd
2 Trebor Road, Pennant Hills, NSW 2120
Printed in Australia by Pirie Printers Pty Limited.